THE
LITTLE
HOUSE
BOOK OF WISDOM

THE LITTLE HOUSE SERIES BY
Laura Ingalls Wilder

Little House in the Big Woods
Farmer Boy
Little House on the Prairie
On the Banks of Plum Creek
By the Shores of Silver Lake
The Long Winter
Little Town on the Prairie
These Happy Golden Years
The First Four Years

THE
LITTLE
HOUSE
BOOK OF WISDOM

Laura Ingalls Wilder

HARPER

An Imprint of HarperCollinsPublishers

This book is set in Stempel Schneidler Light, designed by F.H. Ernst Schneidler,
and Little House Script, a typeface based on Laura Ingalls Wilder's
handwritten correspondence, by Julia Sysmäläinen.

The Little House Book of Wisdom
Copyright © 2017 by Little House Heritage Trust

Library of Congress Control Number: 2016949979
ISBN 978-0-06-247078-2

Typography by Jenna Stempel
17 18 19 20 21   PC/PC   10 9 8 7 6 5 4 3 2 1
❖
First Edition

THE

LITTLE
HOUSE

BOOK OF WISDOM

If enough people think of a thing
and work hard enough at it,
I guess it's pretty nearly bound to happen,
wind and weather permitting.

By the Shores of Silver Lake

The pleasures of youth pass away,
but friendship will blossom forever.

Little Town on the Prairie

Once you begin being naughty,
it is easier to go on and on, and sooner or
later something dreadful happens.

On the Banks of Plum Creek

Have confidence in yourself,
that's the only way to make other folks
have confidence in you.

These Happy Golden Years

A storm outdoors is
no reason for gloom
in the house.

The Long Winter

There is nothing in the world
so good as good neighbors.

On the Banks of Plum Creek

There is no comfort anywhere
for anyone who dreads to go home.

Little Town on the Prairie

Good weather never lasts forever
on this earth.

Little House on the Prairie

To win anything,
we must have the ambition to do so.

These Happy Golden Years

We must not accept hospitality
without making some return.

On the Banks of Plum Creek

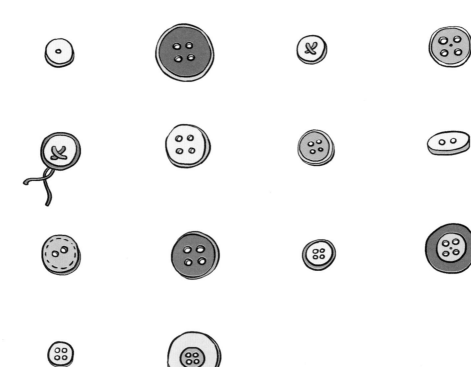

We'd never get anything fixed to suit us
if we waited for things to suit us
before we started.

By the Shores of Silver Lake

The trouble with organizing a thing
is that pretty soon folks get to
paying more attention to the organization
than to what they're organized for.

Little Town on the Prairie

A body makes his own luck,
be it good or bad.

These Happy Golden Years

If you don't want trouble,
don't go looking for it.

On the Banks of Plum Creek

You got to treat folks right or you don't last
long in business, not in this country.

The Long Winter

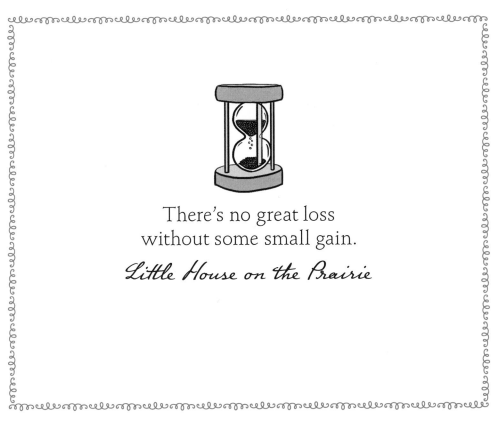

There's no great loss
without some small gain.

Little House on the Prairie

The life of the earth comes up
with a rush in the springtime.

Farmer Boy

Now is now.
It can never be a long time ago.

Little House in the Big Woods

This earthly life is a battle.
If it isn't one thing to contend with,
it's another. It always has been so,
and it always will be. The sooner you make
up your mind to that, the better off you are,
and more thankful for your pleasures.

Little Town on the Prairie

What must be done
is best done cheerfully.

On the Banks of Plum Creek

The last time always seems sad,
but it isn't really. The end of one thing
is only the beginning of another.

These Happy Golden Years

Laura felt a warmth inside her.
It was very small but it was strong.
It was steady, like a tiny light in the dark,
and it burned very low but no winds could
make it flicker because it would not give up.

The Long Winter

Never bet your money
on another man's game.

Farmer Boy

Everything is evened up in this world.
The rich have their ice in summer,
but the poor get theirs in the winter.

The First Four Years

Meet Laura

Laura Ingalls Wilder was born in the Big Woods of Wisconsin on February 7, 1867, to Charles Ingalls and his wife, Caroline.

When Laura was still a baby, Pa and Ma decided to move to a farm near Keytesville, Missouri, and the family lived there about a year. Then they moved to land on the prairie south of Independence, Kansas. After two years in their little house on the prairie, the Ingallses went back to the Big Woods to live in the same house they had left three years earlier.

This time the family remained in the Big Woods for three years. These were the years that Laura wrote about in her first book, *Little House in the Big Woods*.

In the winter of 1874, when Laura was seven, Ma and Pa decided to move west to Minnesota. They found a beautiful farm near Walnut Grove, on the banks of Plum Creek.

The next two years were hard ones for the Ingallses. Swarms of grasshoppers devoured all the crops in the area, and Ma and Pa could not pay off all their debts. The family decided they could no longer keep the farm on Plum Creek, so they moved to Burr Oak, Iowa.

After a year in Iowa, the family returned to Walnut Grove again, and Pa built a house in town and started a butcher shop. Laura was ten years old by then, and she helped earn money for the family by working in the dining room of the hotel in Walnut Grove, babysitting, and running errands.

The family moved only once more, to the little town of De Smet in Dakota Territory. Laura was now twelve and had lived in at least twelve little houses. Laura grew into a young lady in De Smet, and met her husband, Almanzo Wilder, there.

Laura and Almanzo were married in 1885, and

their daughter, Rose, was born in December 1886. By the spring of 1890, Laura and Almanzo had endured too many hardships to continue farming in South Dakota. Their house had burned down in 1889, and their second child, a boy, had died before he was a month old.

First, Laura, Almanzo, and Rose went east to Spring Valley, Minnesota, to live with Almanzo's family. About a year later they moved south to Florida. But Laura did not like Florida, and the family returned to De Smet.

In 1894, Laura, Almanzo, and Rose left De Smet for good and settled in Mansfield, Missouri.

When Laura was in her fifties, she began to write

down her memories of her childhood, and in 1932, when Laura was 65 years old, *Little House in the Big Woods* was published. It was an immediate success, and Laura was asked to write more books about her life on the frontier.

Laura died on February 10, 1957, three days after her ninetieth birthday, but interest in the Little House books continued to grow. Since their first publication so many years ago, the Little House books have been read by millions of readers all over the world.